THE SCHOOLS HISTORY PROJECT

S·H·P

OFFICIAL TEXT

THIS IS HIST

The Norman Conquest

AN INVESTIGATION FOR KEY STAGE 3

CHRISTOPHER CULPIN

IAN DAWSON

JOHN MURRAY

The Schools History Project

The Project was set up in 1972, with the aim of improving the study of history for students aged 13–16. This involved a reconsideration of the ways in which history contributes to the educational needs of young people. The Project devised new objectives, new criteria for planning and developing courses, and the materials to support them. New examinations, requiring new methods of assessment, also had to be developed. These have continued to be popular. The advent of GCSE in 1987 led to the expansion of Project approaches into other syllabuses.

The Schools History Project has been based at Trinity and All Saints College, Leeds, since 1978, from where it supports teachers through a biennial Bulletin, regular INSET, an annual conference and a website (www.tasc.ac.uk/shp).

Since the National Curriculum was drawn up in 1991, the Project has continued to expand its publications, bringing its ideas to courses for Key Stage 3 as well as a range of GCSE and A level specifications.

Words printed in SMALL CAPITALS are defined in the Glossary on page 58.

Layouts by Amanda Hawkes
Artwork by Art Construction, Jon Davis/Linden Artists, Richard Duszczak, Tony Randell, Edward Ripley, Chris Rothero/Linden Artists, Kate Sheppard, Steve Smith
Typeset in Goudy by Wearset Ltd, Boldon, Tyne and Wear
Printed and bound in Dubai by Oriental Press.

A catalogue entry for this book is available from the British Library

ISBN 0 7195 8555 4
Teachers' Resource Book ISBN 0 7195 8556 2

◆ Contents

SECTION 1 THE BATTLE OF HASTINGS

1.1 1066!
Work out why 1066 is such a famous date in English history — 2

1.2 Why did William win the Battle of Hastings?
Five reasons why William beat Harold at Hastings – but which do you think is most important? Write a persuasive paragraph to support your view — 4

1.3 Who was telling the truth about being king?
Explain what you think of William's and Harold's claims to the English throne — 20

1.4 What have you learned about using evidence?
Think about what source testers do with unreliable sources — 26

SECTION 2 DID THE NORMAN CONQUEST CHANGE EVERYTHING?

2.1 Time to rebel?
Decide whether you would have been brave enough (or stupid enough) to rebel against the Normans — 30

2.2 Was the Norman Conquest really so important?
Work out if the Normans changed everything for everybody — 42

2.3 The story of the Norman Conquest
Write your own Norman story — 50

2.4 Could you live in Norman England?
Decide what was good and what was bad about life in Norman England — 54

2.5 What happened next?
Connect the Norman Conquest to the next 1000 years of history — 56

Glossary — 58

Index — 59

Titles in the series and Acknowledgements — 60

DOMESDAY
BOOK

TERRA REGIS
Rex habet burgú Barn
duid. Ibi fő uroa burgú .xl. t
Inrotms redd regi .xl. sol' ds
solid ad numerum. Ibi f' x
ueniu in Augluam.

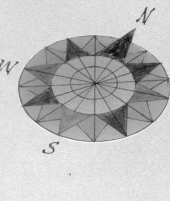

IRELAND

SAXON SOLDIERS

VILLAGERS

NORMAN SOLDIERS

THE BATTLE OF HASTINGS

SCOTLAND

YORK

STAMFORD
BRIDGE

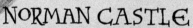

VIKING SHIP

ENGLAND

RIVER HUMBER

KING
HAROLD

NORMAN CASTLE

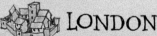

LONDON

ES

PEVENSEY 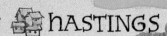 HASTINGS

ENGLISH CHANNEL

WILLIAM
DUKE OF
NORMANDY

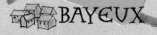 BAYEUX

FRANCE

NORMANDY

1.1 1066!

Work out why 1066 is such a famous date in English history

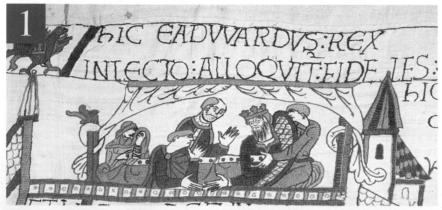

As the famous year 1066 began, Edward the Confessor, king of England, lay dying. Who was to be the next king?

ACTIVITY A

The date 1066 is one of the most famous in British history. Look at the pictures on pages 2–3. As a class, see if you can work out what happened in 1066 and why it is such a famous date.

On the very day that Edward was buried, Harold, Earl of Wessex, was crowned king.

William, Duke of Normandy, thought he was the rightful king and invaded England.

Harold and William fought a battle at Hastings. It lasted all day.

2

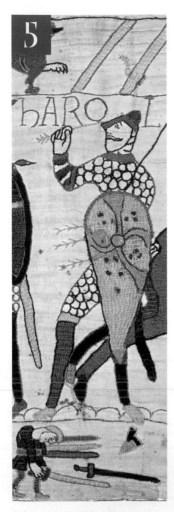

After several hours fighting, Harold was killed.

William was crowned king of England on Christmas Day, 1066.

1 Make a list of questions you want to ask about the Norman Conquest. Some of your questions will probably be **little questions**: interesting, but not about important issues, e.g. Why do William and Harold have different hairstyles? What did they wear under their chain mail? and so on.

Some of your questions will be **big questions**: getting to the heart of why these events are so famous. e.g. Did the Norman Conquest change England's history? Why did William invade England?

2 Sort your questions into these two categories:

◆ little questions
◆ big questions.

The NORMANS built Britain's first castle to keep the English under control.

The Normans seized what they wanted from the English: land, cattle and other possessions.

Five reasons why William beat Harold

◆ The big question

The key event in the Norman Conquest of England in 1066 was the Battle of Hastings. The first big, significant question you are going to answer is therefore:

WHY DID WILLIAM WIN THE BATTLE OF HASTINGS?

We think this is a big, significant question because:

- ◆ William was the last person to invade England and conquer it. In the thousand years since then several other leaders – Napoleon and Hitler for example – have tried. They all failed. So why William succeeded seems to be an important question.
- ◆ We think the Norman Conquest changed English history. You will find out how and why in Section 2 of this book.

Who fought whom at Hastings?
On one side: King Harold, the last ANGLO-SAXON king of England.
On the other: William, Duke of Normandy.

What were they fighting for?
The crown of England – the right to rule one of the richest kingdoms in Europe.

Who won?
William. He became King William I of England.

SOURCE 1

King Harold

Age: 44
Earl of Wessex.
The most powerful man in England, Harold had fought battles all his life. He had fought in Wales and Ireland. He and his brothers controlled most of the country. His sister was married to the old king, Edward. When Edward died early in 1066, Harold was crowned king at once.

SOURCE 2

Duke William

Age: 39
Duke of Normandy.
William was the illegitimate son of the Duke of Normandy and Arlette, a tanner's daughter. He became duke aged eight, when his father died. William had to learn to fight even as a child. His uncles tried to take Normandy from him. On one occasion he had to get up at night and ride away from assassins sent to kill him. He had defeated most of his enemies in battle and by the 1060s was safe in power. He claimed that King Edward had told him he would be the next king.

You are going to write an answer to the big question: why did William win the Battle of Hastings? It will need to be quite long. But don't worry, you are going to get lots of help. The authors of this book are going to write some of it, and you are going to get help and advice from two special assistants.

When historians come up against a big **Why?** question like this, they try to think of possible reasons why, then test their ideas against the evidence and the facts. That is exactly what you are going to do. Historians have come up with five possible reasons why William won. You are going to deal with them one at a time (look for the **Q** logo), then explain what you have found out in a paragraph for each reason.

As you go through this section you will see if the evidence, and the facts, support that idea. The sixth paragraph is for your summing up – your own personal conclusion, having weighed all the evidence and the history.

We'll get you started on each one.

Why did William win the Battle of Hastings?

◆ Paragraph 1: Because William was a good leader?
◆ Paragraph 2: Because Harold was a bad leader?
◆ Paragraph 3: Because Harold rushed into battle?
◆ Paragraph 4: Because William's army was better equipped?
◆ Paragraph 5: Because William outwitted Harold at Hastings?
◆ Paragraph 6: This is the place for your conclusion – your own ideas. You can tackle this by saying which of the five historians' questions you think gets nearest to the best answer and say why you think this.

ACTIVITY

1 Suppose you wanted to find out about a big battle which took place in the last ten years. Which of the types of sources in the table below would you be able to use? Make your own copy of the table then in column 2 tick each one you could probably use.
2 Now think about the Battle of Hastings, in 1066. Which of the items below could you use? Put your ticks in column 3.

Type of source	A battle in the last ten years	The Battle of Hastings, 1066
Eye-witness accounts		
TV programmes		
Newspaper reports		
Books about the battle		
Photographs		
Visible remains at the battle-site		
The diaries and memoirs of those who took part		

◆ *Problems finding out*

There's not much to go on in finding out about the Battle of Hastings. So it's time to meet your first assistant.

I am a Source Tester. You will already know that in history we find out about the past by using sources. But going back a thousand years presents special problems: not many sources have survived and you've got to be very careful how to use the ones that have. Let me show you what I mean. Look first at Source 3.

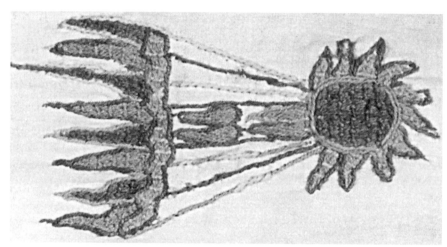

SOURCE 3 This is how the appearance of a COMET was recorded by the embroiderers who made the Bayeux Tapestry. In this picture you can see the actual stitches they made and the different shades of dyed wool they used.

The Bayeux Tapestry is a helpful source. It was made quite soon after the battle. It is full of good pictures and fun to look at. You've seen some of it already (and you're going to see it a lot more!) However, in order to use an historical source, you need to know something about it – who made it, when, why, etc. We call this information the **attribution**. It obviously affects the way we use a source. Is it telling us the truth? Is it telling us the whole truth? In this book the attribution of important sources is put in a special box, like this:

The Bayeux Tapestry
The Bayeux Tapestry was woven in England, not long after 1066. But it was made on the orders of Odo, William's half-brother. It therefore tells a Norman version of the story.

For example, the tapestry has the comet picture just after the picture of Harold's CORONATION. But Harold was crowned in January, a good three months before the comet actually appeared at Easter. The designer of the tapestry changed the timing in order to make it seem as if bad luck followed Harold from the moment he seized the throne.

SOURCE 4 Bishop Odo was a priest; he is shown with a priest's haircut called a tonsure, which was shaved in the middle. He was the Bishop of Bayeux, in Normandy, from which the tapestry gets its name.

Here is Bishop Odo. He is shown on the right, telling William to build ships to get his soldiers to England. The designer wanted to show the boss, Odo, playing a big part in these events.

So you can see that using sources is not quite as simple as it looks. That's where the team comes in: Source Testers 'R' Us will help you sort out the sources. There will also be extra questions marked like this ★ to help you analyse the sources.

SOURCE TESTERS 'R' US
CHECK ALL SOURCES VERY CAREFULLY
WHO   WHY   WHEN

ACTIVITY B

What questions can you ask of the tapestry to which it will give reasonably accurate, trustworthy answers?

Try it on Source 4: what does Source 4 tell us about Odo and William which is reasonably fair and accurate?

ACTIVITY A

Read the attribution box for the Bayeux Tapestry.

Put the Bayeux Tapestry through the quality control checks carried out by Source Testers 'R' Us.

Check 1: WHO?
◆ Who ordered the tapestry to be made?
◆ What is their position?
◆ How might this affect what the tapestry shows?

Check 2: WHY?
◆ Does the tapestry try to make anyone look good?
◆ Does it try to make anyone look bad?
◆ Is it likely to be fair?
◆ Is it likely to be accurate?

Check 3: WHEN?
◆ When was it made?
◆ Did the makers know about, or witness, the events they were portraying?

In conclusion
◆ Give the Bayeux Tapestry a mark out of 5 for its accuracy.
◆ Give it a mark out of 5 for how trustworthy it is.

Tricky, isn't it? But at least you know what you're dealing with now: the good old Bayeux Tapestry may not be completely fair. It may not be completely accurate. That doesn't mean it is useless and we should give up. We haven't got much else to go on for nearly a thousand years ago.

My last word: all historical sources have to be treated like this. You'll see what I mean later, when you have another go at being a Source Tester.

①1 Was William a better leader than Harold?

You are going to use this section to write the first paragraph in your answer to the big question: 'Why did William win the Battle of Hastings?'

What did it mean to be a good army leader in 1066? A good leader had to persuade people to fight for him, and make them feel good about what they were doing. And having got together an army, a good leader had to organise it well. You are going to see how William measured up to these CRITERIA.

1 The eleventh century was a very religious time. People really believed that the side which God supported would be bound to win. William made a big effort to show God was on his side. He got the Pope – the head of the Church – to send his support (see Source 5). This made sure that people thought he was God's choice for king of England, not just a greedy invader.

2 He had a special problem in attacking Harold: Britain is an island, so he would have to get an army, big enough to defeat Harold, and all its supplies, across the Channel. The tapestry shows William making thorough preparations for the invasion: cutting trees; making ships; loading them with food, drink, horses, armour and weapons. Some of these things can be seen in Sources 6 and 7.

The Bayeux Tapestry gives evidence in pictures of William's leadership in 1066. How can we use these pictures as sources of evidence to help us write about William's leadership qualities?

ACTIVITY A

To start off your paragraph about William as a leader, you need to try to bring in the main points from **1** (see left), as well as using, and commenting on, Source 5. You will need to use some good **connectives** (linking words). The paragraph below uses simple listing connectives: firstly, secondly . . . . It also uses a **topic sentence**: a sentence that sets up the paragraph.

> *William was a good leader in two ways. Firstly, he persuaded people to join his army by getting the support of the Church. One scene from the Bayeux Tapestry shows the Pope's flag flying from one of his ships. This is almost certainly accurate. The designer of the tapestry was a Norman and tells the story from a Norman point of view; but this is the kind of detail that would be known by many people and so is probably right. Secondly…*

1 Let's see how this paragraph works. On a copy of the paragraph, underline in red any sentence which makes a simple statement about William in answer to the question 'Was he a good leader?'
2 Underline in blue any sentence which supplies evidence to support these statements about William.
3 Underline in green any comment which shows that the writer has thought about the fairness and accuracy of the evidence.
4 Now write the second part of this paragraph: use **2** (above left) and Sources 6 and 7 to describe to the reader what the tapestry tells you about William's abilities as an organiser and whether this particular evidence is to be trusted.

SOURCE 5 Ship flying the Pope's banner.

SOURCE 6 Shipbuilding.

SOURCE 7 Loading armour and supplies.

Q2 *Was Harold a bad leader?*

Evidence is not just what the sources tell you. You can also look at people's actions in order to help understand their motives. What do the events of 1066 tell us about Harold as leader?

In September 1066, while Harold and his soldiers waited for William on the south coast of England, a huge fleet of 300 ships landed on the coast of Yorkshire. It was led by the most formidable Viking warrior in the whole of Europe: Harald Hardraada. He was a huge man who had hacked up enemies in battles all over Europe. In 1045 he had fought his way to become king of Norway. Now he was intent on grabbing the throne of England and was ready to fight anyone who stood in his way.

The local English lords led an army against the Vikings but were defeated in a battle at Fulford, near York, on 20 September 1066. Harald Hardraada went to York to eat, drink and rest. He knew Harold was miles away, in the south, so he thought he was safe.

Harold seems to have had a good network of messengers. We know this because, as soon as he heard about the invaders, he gathered an army together and moved so fast that he took Harald Hardraada by surprise. He attacked Harald on 25 September at Stamford Bridge and won a tremendous victory. Harald Hardraada was killed, along with hundreds of his men. Only 24 ships were needed to carry away the remnants of the army.

1. Pick out four items from this account which show Harold's qualities as a leader.
2. You are going to write a short paragraph about him, answering the question: 'Was Harold a bad leader?' This time you are not using sources as such, you are using the events. You need to use **careful language**, because the judgements you are making about Harold are based, not on what he said, or even what other people at that time said, but just on what he did. Let us start you off:

   > The events of 1066 **suggest** that Harold was also a good leader. For example, he **seems** to have reacted very fast to the news of the invasion in the north.

   Notice the careful language we have used: we cannot be sure, so we use these words. Here are some more careful language words you could use: **might could perhaps possibly probably**
3. Now complete the paragraph about Harold's leadership, based on the four items you listed in answer to question 1.
4. End the paragraph with a sentence comparing William and Harold as leaders. Which of these three possible endings are you going to choose?

   > William was probably a better leader because…
   > Harold was probably a better leader because…
   > William and Harold were both good leaders because…

Q3 *Did William win because Harold rushed into battle?*

Harold waited all summer on the south coast of England with his army ready. But all summer the wind was against William. The invasion force he had prepared so carefully could not set sail.

Then came the dramatic month of September 1066:

8 September Harold's men asked to go home. They were not full-time soldiers but ordinary farmers and they wanted to get the harvest in. Harold had to agree.

20 September Harald Hardraada defeated the English at the Battle of Fulford.

25 September Harold won his great victory at Stamford Bridge.

27 September The wind changed at last. William set sail and landed in England, at Pevensey, on 28 September with no one there to stop him.

End of September William settled in at Hastings and waited. Harold heard the news and rushed south to London.

WAIT

In time William will run out of supplies and his army, camping outside in winter, will get hungry and ill. Then the Normans can be driven off.

Wait. Our best troops are weary after coming down from Stamford Bridge.

Keep him bottled up in Sussex.

Stop William getting supplies.

You are king; William has to defeat you, not the other way round. William needs to fight, but you do not.

Harold halted at London to decide what to do next. His advisers were divided. Here is what their council meeting might have looked like.

What should Harold do next?

ACTIVITY A

What would this meeting be like? Here is a possible description of the scene as a speaker tries to persuade Harold not to attack William:

> *The first to speak was an old soldier. He stood up to address the King, standing stiffly, partly from his age, partly from the five days he had spent in the saddle riding down from Stamford Bridge.*
>
> *'My lord', he said, bowing slightly, 'You are the King of England. If this Norman duke wants the crown he has to find you and defeat you. At this moment time is on his side: our men are weary and his men are fresh. But the pendulum will swing our way. He only has the men he brought with him on his ships, while you have thousands of men you can call on. Leave him alone for now. Guard the roads and stop him getting supplies from far off. Soon his men will get hungry, ill, while ours will be rested. Then we can drive him back into the sea. I say wait!'*
>
> *The King nodded a little, perhaps in agreement. But then a younger man on the other side of the table began to speak:*

1 Now write what the young man said, using the points made from the other side of the table and Source 8.

2 The speech you have just written, or one like it, won over Harold. He did not wait for reinforcements, but rushed on to meet William. Write the next paragraph of your big writing task: it can be quite short. Begin with the topic sentence: 'William had a better chance of winning because Harold rushed into battle.' Then decide whether you agree or disagree with this statement, and write from your point of view.

FIGHT

> William has built a castle at Pevensey and is terrorising the people of Sussex, burning their houses and seizing their cattle.

> William has to be defeated!

> Gather an army from the people of south-east England. Get down into Sussex and attack William as soon as possible.

> A king is expected to defend his people from attacks like this: you cannot let them down.

> We've just won a great victory – we're on a roll!

SOURCE 8 Normans burning a house. The woman and her son are made homeless – refugees of war.

ACTIVITY B

Source 8 shows the Normans behaving cruelly. Yet it is from the Bayeux Tapestry. Do you think this means it is likely to be accurate? Explain why you think this.

Q4 *Was William's army better equipped?*

SOURCE 10 The Anglo-Saxon shield-wall.

SOURCE 9 Norman soldiers on horseback.

SOURCE 11 Norman archers.

SOURCE 12 Anglo-Saxon soldier with battle-axe.

Harold travelling on horseback.

SOURCE 13 Anglo-Saxon and Norman soldiers, both with swords.

SOURCE 14 From a poem written about 1100, called 'The Song of the Battle of Hastings'.

> The English scorn horses and,
> trusting in their strength,
> fight on foot.

ACTIVITY

1 Weapons. Use this table to list which side used which weapons:

Weapon	Anglo-Saxon	Norman
Helmet		
Chain-link armour		
Spear		
Shield		
Bow and arrow		
Battle-axe		
Sword		
Horses		

2 Use the table to write the fourth paragraph in your answer. The question is: 'Was William's army better equipped?'

   This time you will need to choose an opening sentence of your own. Remember to comment first on how we know about equipment used at Hastings, and how trustworthy the sources are for answering this question. Then give your decision in answer to the question, with reasons.

Q5 *Did William outwit Harold at Hastings?*

William built an abbey here after the conquest.

At last we come to the battle.

As William rode up to meet Harold's army on the morning of 14 October 1066, he knew he had to win the battle. But to win decisively he also had to kill Harold. A win with Harold still alive, and able to gather together another army, would be no good.

What have you decided about the two sides so far? Were they more or less even? Did the Normans have a slight advantage? If they did, it was outweighed by the position Harold took up: he and his housecarls, the closest warriors sworn to fight to the death for their king, were positioned on the crest of a low hill – see Source 16.

The Anglo-Saxon soldiers lined up along the crest of the hill.

The Normans had to charge up the hill.

SOURCE 16 Artist's impression of how the two sides lined up at the Battle of Hastings and, inset top left, a recent photograph of where the battle is said to have taken place.

The battle lasted nine hours. This is quite unusual, and tells us that there was no great difference between the two sides. On these pages we are going to give an overview of the whole battle, in three phases, then look at the key turning point in more detail.

Overview

Phase 1 The early Norman attack

ACTIVITY

As you read the overview, think about who seemed to be winning at the end of each phase.

SOURCE 17

The Normans charged up the hill.

SOURCE 18

The Anglo-Saxon shield-wall held against them.

SOURCE 19

Many Normans, and their horses, were killed. They had to pull back.

Phase 2 The turning point

The Normans charged again then turned and pretended to run away.

The Anglo-Saxons broke from their line and ran down the hill after them.

Then the Normans suddenly turned round and attacked the disorganised Anglo-Saxons. Many were killed.

Phase 3 The end of the Anglo-Saxons

The Normans attacked the reduced Anglo-Saxon line again and again.

Harold's brothers were killed.

Norman archers fired their arrows.

Harold was killed with an arrow in his eye.

With nothing left to fight for, the last Anglo-Saxon warriors fought on for a while, then fled.

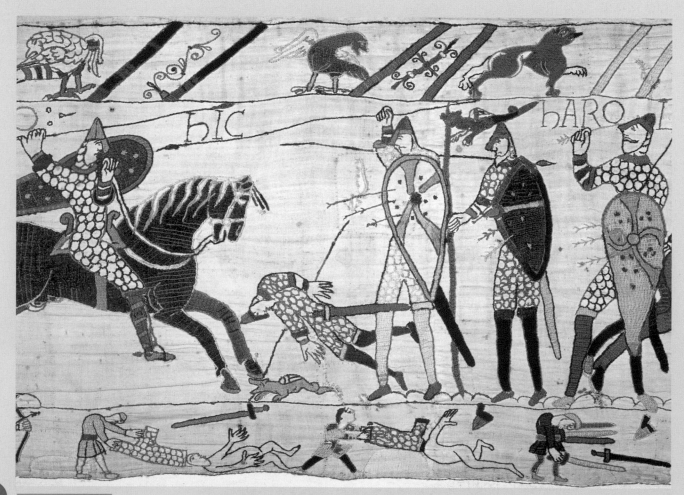

SOURCE 20 Harold (on the right) killed by an arrow in his eye.

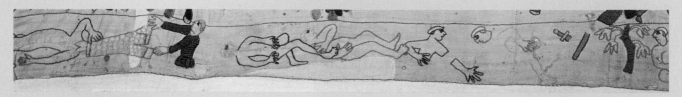

SOURCE 21 Stealing from the dead.

After the battle

Night fell. Thieves crept on to the battlefield to steal from the dead and dying. Edith Swanneck, the beautiful Irish girl who had become Harold's lifetime partner and mother of his children, came looking for him among the corpses. Only she could recognise his body. She had it taken away and buried at Waltham, the abbey Harold had founded. The last Anglo-Saxon king was dead.

William and his Normans were masters of England.

The turning point: the running away

Historians are not really sure why William won this long, closely fought battle. One possible reason was that the Normans pretended to run away, so that the English broke ranks and pursued them. The Normans are then supposed to have turned and re-grouped themselves, attacking the surprised English. But is this possible?

◆ It would involve a lot of men acting together. Modern experts say this would be too hard to organise without modern communication methods such as radios.

But on the other hand:

◆ It was a common tactic at that time. It had been used by the Normans at the Battle of Arques, in 1053. Walter Giffard was at Arques and was one of William's commanders at Hastings.

ACTIVITY

1 From what you have been told here, do you think the pretended running away is: impossible/unlikely/likely/definite?

   Notice that we don't have a straight yes/no choice: history is like that. Sometimes the questions haven't got straight answers. That doesn't mean we give up: we just need a wider range of words to say exactly what we mean.

2 Now write the fifth paragraph in your long answer. The question is: 'Did William outwit Harold at Hastings?' Use the word or words you have chosen above in a short paragraph giving your decision on this question.

> Our view is that they did pretend to run away. Perhaps small groups of men, about 20 or 30 at a time did it. It only needed some of the English to break ranks and run down the hill for the shield-wall to be severely weakened. Do you agree?

◆ Conclusion

So why **did** William win the battle of Hastings? We've looked
at the key events of 1066: what is your conclusion?

ACTIVITY

1 The first stage in coming to your own
conclusion is to prioritise. This means sorting
out the items you have been given according to
their importance. Start by rating the five
possible factors we have been looking at as:
- ◆ not true
- ◆ true but unimportant
- ◆ important but not vital
- ◆ vital.

The five factors are:
- ◆ William was a better leader
- ◆ Harold was a bad leader
- ◆ Harold lost because he rushed into battle
- ◆ William was better equipped
- ◆ William outwitted Harold on the battlefield.

2 Use your rating as you read the conclusion
below, which the authors of this book have
written. On a copy of the conclusion, underline
in blue all the statements that you agree with.
Underline in red all the statements you think are
untrue or unfair.

> William won because he was the better leader.
> He got the Church to support him, so that
> people felt God was on their side. He organised
> the Norman invasion force very quickly and
> successfully. Harold was not such a good
> leader. He was too impulsive and rushed into
> things. He shouldn't have rushed down to
> fight William in 1066, but waited for William
> to hit problems. William's army was also better
> equipped, with cavalry horses and more
> archers. This gave him victory without having
> to resort to difficult tactics like pretending to
> retreat and then turning around.

This conclusion is far too definite as it stands.
Where are 'probably', 'perhaps' and 'possibly'?
Add one or more of these words to improve
this conclusion.

Either:

3 Now it's your turn: see if you can do better in
writing your own conclusion. The place to start
is your list of priority ratings from question 1.
Probably different people in the class will come
up with different lists. That's fine: history is like
that. On big questions like this one there is no
'right answer' that the whole class is struggling
to find. It's not a maths lesson. But you will
have to defend your decision: history isn't a
guessing game, either. Good luck!

Or:

4 You could choose this task. It uses the five
questions we asked as the basis for five reports
to someone who really cared about the answers.
For this option you can work in groups and write
one report each or on your own and write all five.
Look at Source 22 and use all you have found
out in this section to write a report for King
Malcolm. The report should be short and clear.

Spy 1 Was William a good leader?
Spy 2 Was Harold a bad leader?
Spy 3 Did William win because Harold rushed
into battle?
Spy 4 Did William win because the Normans
were better equipped?
Spy 5 Did William outwit Harold at Hastings?

Then write a final paragraph telling King
Malcolm the most important reason Harold lost.

SOURCE 22 Scotland in 1066 was a separate country. Nevertheless, the King of Scotland, Malcolm III, must have watched events in England with some anxiety: was Scotland going to be the Normans' next conquest? He sent five spies to England to find out all he could about what happened, so he could be ready to defeat William.

King Malcolm asked me to find out if William was a good leader.

I had to see if Harold was a bad leader.

Here's my report on whether William won because Harold rushed into battle.

The King asked me to find out if the Norman army was better equipped.

He asked me to report on whether William outwitted Harold at Hastings.

SOURCE TESTERS 'R' US

RATING

Congratulations on working out why William won and starting to write about sources.
Now I'm going to set you some real puzzles to work on . . .

William's and Harold's claims to the English throne

When we used the Bayeux Tapestry to find out about the events of 1066, I warned you about its trustworthiness, its accuracy. On the whole, the tapestry was able to give you quite trustworthy information in response to the kind of questions we asked – about ships, weapons, tactics, etc. But what if a source gives untrustworthy answers to a question? What can you say? Do you just throw it in the source bin and ignore it? That is what we are going to investigate in this unit. The problem was that both William and Harold said they were the rightful king of England. They couldn't both be right. Who was telling the truth?

◆ What was William's story?

We have seen that old King Edward was keen to have William as his HEIR. William also regarded himself as the rightful king of England because of something which had happened not long before, in 1064.

According to William, Edward sent Harold to Normandy. He was shipwrecked, then rescued by Duke William. In Source 1, William of Poitiers describes what happened while Harold was staying with William.

SOURCE 1

William . . . took Harold with proper honour to Rouen. There William sumptuously refreshed Harold with splendid hospitality after all the hardships of his journey. For the duke rejoiced to have so illustrious a guest in a man who had been sent him by the nearest and dearest of his friends. One, moreover, who was in England second only to the King, and who might prove a faithful helper between him and the English . . . . And as is testified by the most truthful and most honourable men who were there present, he took an OATH of his own free will in the following terms:

Firstly, that he would be the representative of Duke William at the court of his lord, King Edward, as long as the King lived.

Secondly, that he would employ all his influence and wealth to ensure that after the death of King Edward the kingdom of England should be confirmed in the possession of the Duke.

SOURCE 2 Harold taking the oath, from the Bayeux Tapestry. William is on the left, on his throne. Harold has his hands resting on two altars (one of them portable) which contained the bones of saints. People at the time regarded an oath taken in this way as specially powerful. The tapestry shows the oath being taken at Bayeux. It does not say what Harold promised in the oath.

If these sources are telling the truth, then Harold was in a very weak position: breaking such an oath was a very serious act at that time – he deserved to die.

ACTIVITY

State briefly what William said about his claim to the throne of England.

Evaluating the sources for William's story

Sometimes we can tell the point of view of a writer without knowing about the attribution, just from the attitudes expressed. (We call this 'reading between the lines' or **inference**.)

1 What is the attitude of William of Poitiers, the writer of Source 1, towards William?

2 Which **adjectives** and **adverbs** does William of Poitiers use which give him away? On your own copy, underline them.

3 What would happen if you changed these words? For example, change the underlined words to make it seem as if he disliked William.

4 What do you think the artist who designed Source 2 is trying to tell us about this event?

Before you accept William's story, you need to use my Source Testers on the two sources you have seen. You know about the Bayeux Tapestry. What about this William of Poitiers?

William of Poitiers
William of Poitiers was a Norman. Source 1 is taken from a book he wrote in the 1070s called *The Deeds of William Duke of the Normans and King of the English*. He was William's personal priest.

Is William's version of the oath story based on trustworthy evidence?

Soon you will be asked to write about the trustworthiness of some different evidence, so let's see how the authors of this book approach William's version:

> The story of Harold's oath seems to be based only on Norman sources. They would be bound to support William's version of events. After all, William needed to prove that he was the rightful king of England. The Bayeux Tapestry was made for William's half-brother, Odo. William of Poitiers was an admirer of William and his personal priest. We cannot trust these particular sources to tell us the whole truth about the oath.

If we cannot trust these sources, what can we say about them?

> The Bayeux Tapestry and William of Poitiers' account may not be trustworthy for telling us whether the oath took place in the way William said it did. However, they do tell us what William wanted people to believe about it.

◆ *What was the English story?*

When you have one or more sources which are obviously BIASED for one side, as the Bayeux Tapestry and William of Poitiers are, it is sometimes helpful to look for sources from the other side. So, what do the English sources say about the oath?

SOURCE 3 *The Anglo-Saxon Chronicle.* This recorded events in England over the years. Although there is nothing for the year 1064, for the year 1066 one version of the *Chronicle* says:

> *. . . the wise ruler [Edward] entrusted the realm*
> *To a man of high rank, to Harold himself,*
> *A **noble** earl who all the time*
> *Had **loyally** followed his lord's commands*
> *With words and deeds, and **neglected nothing***
> *That met the needs of the people's king.*

SOURCE 4 Another English chronicle, called after the person who probably wrote it, John of Worcester, describes some events in 1064, but does not mention the oath. For 1066, John says:

> *After his [Edward's] burial, the under-king, Harold, son of Earl Godwin, whom the King had nominated as his successor, was chosen king by the leading nobles of all England; and on the same day Harold was crowned with great ceremony . . . . On taking the helm of the kingdom, Harold immediately began to abolish unjust laws and to make good ones; to patronise churches and monasteries; to pay particular reverence to bishops, abbots, monks . . . and to show himself pious, humble and friendly to all good men. But he treated criminals with great severity and gave orders to his earls and sheriffs to imprison all thieves, robbers and disturbers of his kingdom. He laboured . . . by sea and by land for the protection of his realm.*

The next king could be a relative of the last king

But this person could be set aside if not suitable

The next king has to be a person of good personal character

The next king has to be chosen by the leading people of the country

SOURCE 5 A Saxon king and leading nobles.

ACTIVITY

What, then, was the English story? Use Sources 3, 4 and 5 and your knowledge of how people became king at that time to write a brief account of how Harold saw the events of 1066.

But can we trust these sources? Let's see the attributions.

RATING

The Anglo-Saxon Chronicle
In the 870s, King Alfred ordered that a record of events, year by year, should be kept. This became known as *The Anglo-Saxon Chronicle*. As the only literate people at that time were in the Church, it was written by monks. Several monasteries kept their own versions. Source 3 is from a version probably made in northern England in the late eleventh century.

John of Worcester
This is another chronicle kept by a monk. The early parts are the same as *The Anglo-Saxon Chronicle*, but John wrote his own account of the years we are interested in.

1
Read between the lines: what is the attitude of Source 3 towards Harold? Note especially the words we have highlighted in **bold**.

2
What is the attitude of Source 4 towards Harold? Look for adjectives, adverbs or verbs that express an opinion.

3
Can we trust Sources 3 and 4? The trustworthiness of a source can change if you change the question. Suppose we ask of these two sources:
a) Are they trustworthy evidence about Harold?
b) Are they trustworthy evidence about what people in England thought about Harold becoming king?

4
Explain why you get different answers if you ask different questions.

5
Use what the authors wrote about the Norman sources on page 21 to help you write about the trustworthiness of the English version of events in Sources 3 and 4.

◆ So who was telling the truth?

We have found out that nothing is certain about the answer to this question. We need to use careful, cautious language. This is how a history professor, D. C. Douglas, put it when he was writing about these events:

SOURCE 6 From *William the Conqueror*, by Professor D. C. Douglas.

In 1064 . . . Harold set sail from Bosham in Sussex on a mission to Europe. Almost every detail of his ensuing adventures . . . has been the subject of controversy and no finality can be claimed for any single interpretation . . . .

So far, so good. Professor Douglas then goes on to give his account of what happened. Here are some extracts:

SOURCE 7

A

Following the three earliest accounts* of these events which have survived, it may, however, seem reasonable to suggest that Harold had been commanded [by Edward] to proceed to Normandy . . . to confirm . . . the grant of the succession to the English throne which had . . . been made by the king to the duke.

B

It is impossible not to admire the high competence of William's policy in 1063–1064 . . . or the manner in which it was steadfastly directed towards the eventual fulfilment of his English purpose.

C

On the morrow of the Confessor's death – on the very day of the funeral – Harold . . . had himself crowned as king . . . . The indecent haste of these proceedings indicates that Harold's seizure of the throne was premeditated and that he feared opposition.

(*Professor Douglas explains that the three earliest accounts are the Bayeux Tapestry and the accounts written by William of Poitiers and William of Jumièges, a Norman monk.)

1
What sources is Professor Douglas using?

2
Is he wise to rely on these three sources? What advice would you give the Professor?

3
On a copy of the extracts, use a red pen to underline the words he uses which give away his opinion of William in Source 7B.

4
Use a blue pen to underline the words he uses which give away his opinion of Harold's action in Source 7C.

5
Can you rewrite Source 7C **either** in a way which shows you approve of what Harold did, **or** in a way which reveals no opinion at all?

ACTIVITY

Can you do better than Professor Douglas? Who did have the best right to the throne of England in 1066? Write your answer to these six questions:

1 Why was the oath important?
2 Why is it hard to get at what really happened?
3 What did William say about the oath?
4 What did the English say about the oath?
5 Do you think Harold really took an oath to support William's claim to the throne?
6 Do you think Harold was wrong to be crowned king when Edward died?

How to handle unreliable sources

We ask a question about the past, then we find some evidence that we think might be useful. What do we do with it?

Our evidence-processing facility looks like this:

Is this source trustworthy?

START
Source

SOURCE TESTING MACHINE

NO
It is not trustworthy

YES
it is trustworthy

For a source of this age, 'Yes' is very unlikely. Look more closely at the source and try Source Testers 'R' Us again.

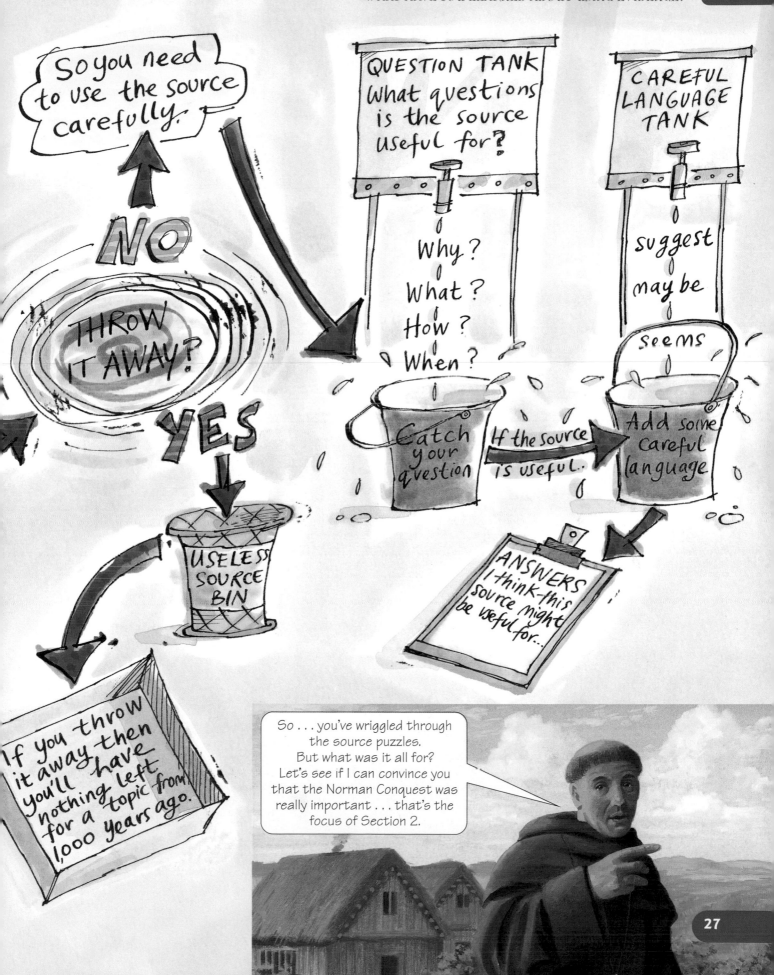

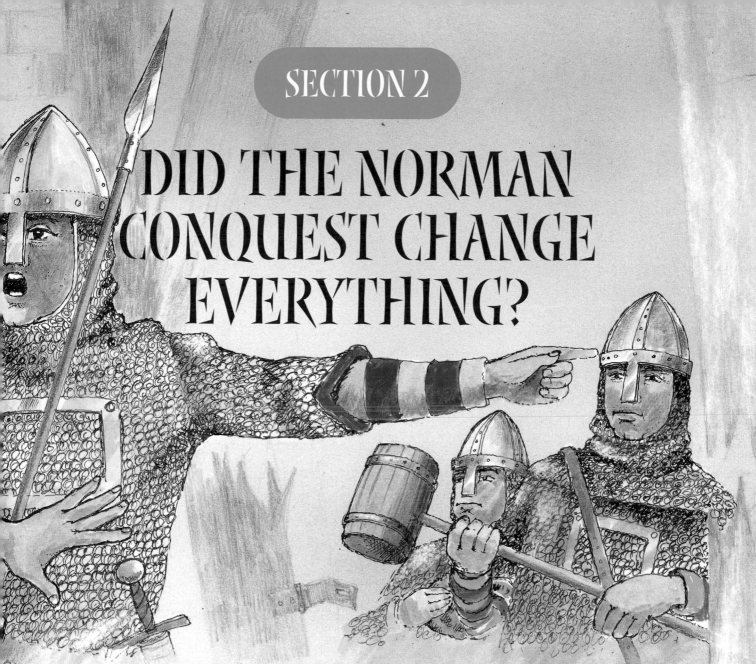

SECTION 2

DID THE NORMAN CONQUEST CHANGE EVERYTHING?

In Section 1 you learned about using sources as you discovered how William became King of England. In Section 2 you will practise more important historical skills as you find out how the Normans took control of England and how they changed it.

Unit 2.1 will teach you about investigating the feelings and attitudes of people in the past. This is what makes history different from other subjects. Only history investigates the lives and feelings of real, individual people.

The investigation of feelings and attitudes is called empathy. Empathy does not mean just imagining what people thought or felt – that's the sort of imaginative work you do writing a story in English. In history you have to use evidence to work out what people thought. In

Unit 2.1, your big question is 'How did the English feel about the Norman invaders?'

That might sound easy – but there's a catch. Most people could not write in 1066 so there aren't many documents to tell us what they were thinking. We have to use other evidence to fill the gaps. What other kinds of evidence could there be?

In Unit 2.2, your big question is 'Was the Norman Conquest really so important?' We all remember 1066 but is that just because of the sound of the words 'ten sixty six' or because the Norman Conquest really was a significant event? In Unit 2.2 you will learn how to decide whether an event like the Norman Conquest was really significant – or just interesting.

King William is dead. The news has just reached us, here in our monastery. It is difficult to believe the King is dead. He has been so powerful, so victorious, since he killed Harold at Hastings, twenty-one years ago.

You won't be surprised to hear that King William died fighting, at war with the King of France. He had just captured a French town and burned it as a warning to his enemy. That was typical William, as ruthless as ever. But, as he rode in triumph through the town, a spark of burning wood fell beneath his horse's hooves. The frightened horse reared up and threw King William back and then violently forward. The iron POMMEL on his saddle drove into his stomach, injuring him so badly that he died a few weeks later.

As soon as the King died, his servants stole his jewels and clothes, leaving his body as naked as if he had been a beggar. Worse was to come. At his funeral the stone coffin was too small for his swollen body but they tried to cram him into it anyway. As they pushed and tugged, his body burst, causing a terrible stinking smell throughout the great cathedral. The nobles and bishops ran out into the fresh air, leaving a handful of monks to bury this great king, William the Conqueror.

The Anglo-Saxon Chronicle was begun in the reign of King Alfred the Great (870–99), two hundred years before Duke William of Normandy conquered England. Several monasteries kept their own versions, adding their own details of events. In 1066 two monasteries were still keeping their chronicle up to date. Here you can see the preface to the Abingdon edition of the Chronicle.

CYNINE SCEAL RICE HEALDAN

So, the King is dead. I must now write about King William and sum up his time as king because I am the chronicler at this monastery.

While I go peacefully about my writing, you and all other English people have a decision to make. They say King William's sons and their lords are fighting among themselves over the crown of England. While they are arguing, this could be our last chance to throw these Normans out of our country. No one has dared to rebel for years because King William was so tough and ruthless. We were afraid of him but now he is dead.

What will you decide to do? Will you rebel and fight? Or will you accept the new Norman king and give up all hope of having an English king again?

ACTIVITY

1 As you work through pages 32–39 complete a table like the one below to collect evidence about whether to rebel or to live peacefully under the Norman king and his lords.

Reasons to rebel against the Normans	Reasons to live in peace with the Normans

2 What do you need to know to help you decide? Make a list of questions you want to ask about events and life since William became king in 1066.

3 Think back over what you have already learned about William and the Normans. Is there anything from earlier in this book that you can put into your table?

◆ How did the Normans try to control the English?

William and his Norman soldiers had a big problem in 1066, even after they had killed King Harold at Hastings. There were only 10,000 of them and there were around 2 million English people. That's 200 English people to every Norman soldier! How could the Normans stop 2 million people from winning back their country?

SOURCE 2 A reconstruction drawing of the castle built at Totnes in Devon in 1068. There were many different styles of MOTTE and BAILEY castles so they did not all look exactly like this one. More evidence is being discovered every year thanks to ARCHAEOLOGICAL digs at early castles. Recent discoveries show that some mottes were covered in timber and that the timber was plastered over to look like stone.

castle

motte

bailey

The Normans built castles throughout England. They were simple castles, usually with a wooden tower on top of a mound called a motte. Most mottes were not very high. Seventy per cent were less than 5 metres tall. Next to the motte was an area called the bailey where the soldiers lived, stored their weapons and stabled their war-horses. It was vital for the Normans to protect their war-horses. The horses gave the Normans a great advantage. A Norman knight on horseback, with his shield and chain mail armour, could cut through enemy foot soldiers like a modern tank but, without their horses, the Norman knights were much less powerful.

The Normans used their castles as bases for controlling the nearby areas. They could ride out from the castles to deal with trouble or retreat into them if they were attacked. By 1087, when William the Conqueror died, the Normans had built around a hundred of these castles. Some were on the coasts to guard against attacks from the kings of Scotland or Denmark but most were in the large towns. These castles were so important that the Normans destroyed many houses to make way for them. William's own Domesday Survey (which you'll find out about on pages 35 and 36) tells us that 166 houses were destroyed in Lincoln, 98 in Norwich and 51 in Shrewsbury. In York, the Normans destroyed nearly 300 houses so they could build two castles because the most dangerous rebellions took place around York in the North.

The English had to get used to the castles and seeing troops of heavily-armed Norman knights riding through their towns and villages. These men were their new lords, men who spoke a different language, men who had the power of life or death over them.

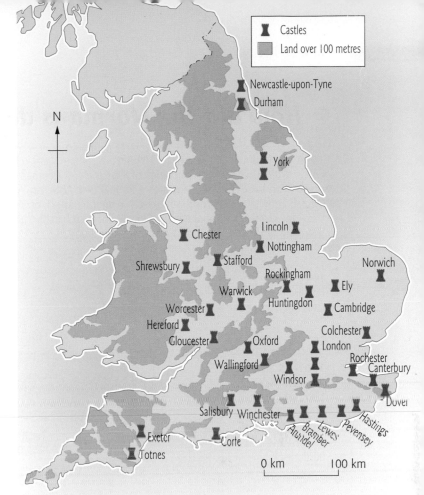

SOURCE 3 Early Norman castles were built in these towns so the Normans could dominate the English.

ACTIVITY

You will not be able to find all the answers to these questions on this page. You need to think and work out some of them for yourself, using the information on this page for clues.

1 Why did the Normans build
  a) so many castles in towns?
  b) the first castles of wood?
  c) most mottes less than 5 metres high?
2 What do the castles tell you about what the Normans thought of the English?
3 'English people hated the Normans after 1066.'
  a) What evidence would you use to support this statement?
  b) Why doesn't that evidence definitely prove that the statement is correct?
  c) What sources would you need to prove definitely that the statement is correct?
4 Start filling in your table from page 31. What reasons can you find on this page to rebel or to live peacefully?

◆ *How did the Normans deal with rebels?*

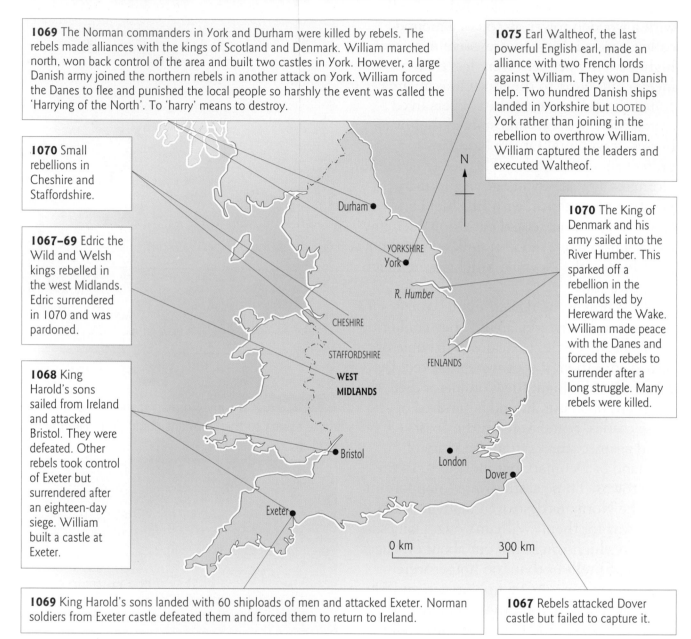

1069 The Norman commanders in York and Durham were killed by rebels. The rebels made alliances with the kings of Scotland and Denmark. William marched north, won back control of the area and built two castles in York. However, a large Danish army joined the northern rebels in another attack on York. William forced the Danes to flee and punished the local people so harshly the event was called the 'Harrying of the North'. To 'harry' means to destroy.

1070 Small rebellions in Cheshire and Staffordshire.

1067–69 Edric the Wild and Welsh kings rebelled in the west Midlands. Edric surrendered in 1070 and was pardoned.

1068 King Harold's sons sailed from Ireland and attacked Bristol. They were defeated. Other rebels took control of Exeter but surrendered after an eighteen-day siege. William built a castle at Exeter.

1075 Earl Waltheof, the last powerful English earl, made an alliance with two French lords against William. They won Danish help. Two hundred Danish ships landed in Yorkshire but LOOTED York rather than joining in the rebellion to overthrow William. William captured the leaders and executed Waltheof.

1070 The King of Denmark and his army sailed into the River Humber. This sparked off a rebellion in the Fenlands led by Hereward the Wake. William made peace with the Danes and forced the rebels to surrender after a long struggle. Many rebels were killed.

1069 King Harold's sons landed with 60 shiploads of men and attacked Exeter. Norman soldiers from Exeter castle defeated them and forced them to return to Ireland.

1067 Rebels attacked Dover castle but failed to capture it.

All the English rebellions failed. Why?

1 There was no strong English leader for the rebels to support as an alternative king to William.
2 The rebellions were not co-ordinated, so William could deal with one before the next one started.
3 The Danes did not want to stop William being king. They were just interested in grabbing as much loot as possible.

4 Most English people did not rebel.
5 William's army was good at dealing with trouble and he dealt harshly with rebels. His castles were good defences for his soldiers.

Even though all these rebellions failed, the northern rebellion in 1069 was a great threat to William. Source 4 on page 35 gives one writer's description of William's 'Harrying of the North'.

SOURCE 4 From a history written by Orderic Vitalis. Orderic was born near Shrewsbury in England in 1075. He had an English mother and Norman father. He was sent to live in Normandy when he was a boy. He became a monk in Normandy and wrote his history around 1125.

King William ordered officers to repair the castles in York. He himself combed the forests and hills, determined to hunt out the enemy hidden there. He killed many people, destroyed the camps of others, harried the land and burned homes to ashes. Nowhere else had William been so cruel. He punished the innocent as much as the guilty. In his anger he commanded that all crops and herds of animals, property and food should be burned so that the whole region north of the Humber would be stripped of all ways of making a living. As a result, a terrible FAMINE fell on the people so that more than 100,000 people died of hunger. I have often praised William, but for this act, which killed innocent as well as guilty by slow starvation, I cannot support him.

SOURCE 5 Extracts from the Domesday Book recording the value of some lands in Yorkshire. The information for the Domesday Survey was collected in 1086, sixteen years after the Harrying of the North. Between 1070 and 1086 there had been raids by Scottish armies in Yorkshire.

Garforth. Value before 1066, 60 shillings, now 30 shillings.

Shippen and Sturton. Value before 1066, 80 shillings, now waste.

Leeds. Value before 1066, 120 shillings, now 140 shillings.

Headingley. Value before 1066, 40 shillings, now 4 shillings.

Also Allerton, Great and Little Preston, Swillington, Skelton, Coldcotes, Colton, Austhorpe, Manston, Potterton, Gipton, Parlington are all waste.

ACTIVITY

1 Fill in your own copy of this table with the details of the rebellion that you think was the most dangerous to William.

Date of rebellion	Part of country	Why was the rebellion dangerous to William?	What was the Normans' reaction?

2 Read Source 4 and use Source Testers (page 7). How trustworthy do you think Source 4 is on the way William punished the North?

3 Read Source 5. Does this support the evidence in Source 4 about William's punishment of the North? Remember to use a word such as definitely, probably or possibly in your answer.

4 Choose two pieces of evidence on these pages that help you to understand English attitudes to the Normans. (Remember that evidence does not just come from what people say in sources – it can also be what people do.) Explain exactly what each piece of evidence tells you.

5 Now fill in more of your table from page 31. Do these past rebellions make you keen to rebel or to live peacefully?

◆ What can we learn from the Domesday Book?

By 1087, when William died, there were only a handful of Englishmen who were still important landowners. William had given all the rest of England to his supporters. However, William did not plan to do that in 1066. At first he only gave his followers the lands of men who had been killed at Hastings. He hoped that if he let English lords keep their lands then they would not rebel.

William changed his mind after all the rebellions against him. He realised that he could not trust the English to stay loyal to him. He decided that the safest way to control England was to take the land away from the English and give it to his own men. That was why William parcelled out English lands to his followers between 1070 and 1080.

We know how the Normans took over from English landowners because, in 1085, William ordered a great investigation that covered the whole of England. This was the Domesday Survey. Here is what an Anglo-Saxon chronicler said about the survey:

SOURCE 6

The King sent his men all over England, into every SHIRE and had them find out how much land the King, the bishops and the lords had in each county and how much that land was worth. So very detailed was this investigation that there was no land, no ox, no cow, no sheep nor one pig left out (I am ashamed to write this but he was not ashamed to do it), and all these records were brought to him.

Why did William order the Domesday Survey? Historians are not sure! There are no documents in which William explained his reasons. William may have wanted better information for raising taxes and feeding his army more efficiently. A second possible reason is that William had granted bits and pieces of land to his lords and bishops over the years and now nobody knew in detail who held which land. This could lead to arguments or fighting, so perhaps William ordered the survey to sort out once and for all who had what land and what taxes each man should pay.

Collecting the information for the Domesday Survey was a huge task but took less than a year. The diagram shows how it was done quickly and efficiently. The Normans used the old Anglo-Saxon administrative system that was very efficient.

1 King William sends his commissioners to gather information for his survey

2 The commissioners ask detailed questions about people and animals in every village

3 The reports are returned to William

4 A scribe writes up all the reports in the Domesday Book

ACTIVITY

1 What was the attitude of the chronicler (Source 6) to the Domesday Survey?

2 Which of his words and phrases support your answer?

3 From Source 6, make a list of the questions you think the commissioners asked.

4 Now use Source 8 to answer those questions for the village of Kennett.

5 Do you think that the people of Kennett had the same attitude as the chronicler in Source 6 to the Domesday Survey?

6 What can you add to your table from page 31? Would the Domesday Survey make you want to rebel – or not?

SOURCE 7 A page from the Domesday Book showing the entry for Kennett and other villages. There are actually two Domesday Books: *Little Domesday*, which contains information about East Anglia; and *Great Domesday*, which covers the rest of the country apart from Cumbria, Durham and Northumberland, which were left out of the survey.

Kennett was taxed in the time of King Edward on 3½ hides of land. It is now taxed on 2½ hides of land. It is held by William de Warenne. There are 5 ploughs on the lord's land and 7 villagers have another 5 ploughs. There are 12 slaves, a mill, a meadow and pasture for all the village animals. In all it is worth 12 pounds. When William received it, it was worth 9 pounds. In the time of King Edward it was held by Tochil, a lord of King Edward, and it was worth 12 pounds.

SOURCE 8 A translation of the entry in the Domesday Book for Kennett in Cambridgeshire. This is the final version after all the information had been collected, then edited down to the essentials. An earlier version recorded that there were 8 cattle, 480 sheep, 10 pigs and 4 horses in Kennett. It also gave the names of the local men who gave evidence to William's commissioners. (A hide was a measurement of land, equal to 120 acres.)

◆ Will the English rebel again?

a Why should I rebel? Most things in the village have not changed at all. We still farm in the same way, live in the same houses and wear the same clothes. The Normans haven't changed what I eat or drink.

b You're wrong. They have changed what we can eat. We need to hunt for food but these new Norman forest laws say only the King and his lords are allowed to hunt deer and other animals. We are not even allowed to collect wood for our fires.

c And if you are caught with a weapon in the forest then they cut off two of your fingers to make sure you can never draw a bow again. The second time they put your eyes out. These Normans think deer are more important than English people but it's different if it's one of them. If a Norman is found dead then everyone in the area has to pay a large fine.

i And it feels safer to travel to fairs and markets. These Norman soldiers keep us merchants safe from thieves, at least down here in the South.

h But they are rebuilding cathedrals too, making them larger. King William was very religious and gave a lot of money to churches. Rebuilding cathedrals is a good way to worship God.

g And they knocked down people's homes to build their castles. They just build them to intimidate us. I hate castles and I hate watching Norman soldiers ride past. They're so arrogant. They look at you and talk and you don't know what they're saying.

f They are ruthless, all right. What about all the places they have destroyed? They've forced people to leave their homes so they can make their new forests. They've burned villages all across the North. Refugees have been begging food from monks in the South.

e But these Normans can do anything they like! Why are they asking all these questions about our village? They are even counting every sheep and pig. Are they going to collect even more taxes or take our animals back to their farms in Normandy?

d There's more important things than forest laws or even Normans. What about the terrible illnesses and great storms we've had this year? In some places the harvest was so poor that people starved to death. That's much worse than a new Norman lord.

Punishments for crimes

Cruelty

Castles

Poor harvests

Security

Forest laws

Domesday Survey

Daily life

Religion

ACTIVITY

This is your last chance to add new information or ideas to your table from page 31.

1 Read what the English villagers are saying.
   a) Match each of the comments to one of the topics illustrated on this page.
   b) Which villagers are complaining?
   c) Which villagers are praising the Normans?
2 Now complete your table. You will have the chance to make your own decision whether to rebel or live in peace when you reach page 41.

Now that you know a lot more about what happened in William's reign, what do you think I should put in my summary? You could even write your own, say about 100 words, and then compare it with mine later.

◆ Time to decide!

I have finished writing about King William. This is what I said about him. Part of it is set out as a poem.

King William was a very wise and powerful man. He was greater and stronger than all the kings before him. He was kind to the good men who served God. During his reign, the great cathedral at Canterbury was built and so were many others throughout England. He was terribly stern to anyone who disobeyed him and he even put lords and his own brother in prison.

We must not forget the good order he kept in the country. A rich man with a bag of gold could travel unharmed right through the country. No man dared to kill another, no matter what evil the other had done to him.

The King was a tough man and greedy.
He forced the poor to build castles.
He took many gold coins from his people,
And many more hundreds of pounds in silver.
He marked out huge forests for deer and made laws about hunting.
Anyone who killed a stag or a doe was to be blinded.
He loved the stags so dearly
As if he was their father.
The rich complained and the poor wept,
But he was too merciless to care if everyone hated him.
They had to obey him,
Or they lost their lives and their lands,
And their goods and the King's friendship.
May Almighty God show mercy to his soul,
And grant him forgiveness for his sins.

ACTIVITY A

1 Make two lists:
   a) the things about William that the chronicler praises
   b) the things he complains about.
2 Do you think this Anglo-Saxon chronicler is giving historians today good evidence about William the Conqueror?
   a) Use the Source Testers check on page 7 to help you decide by putting the chronicle through the quality control checks. Give the chronicler a reliability rating out of 5.
   b) Justify your rating by writing a paragraph explaining which checks the chronicle passed and which it failed.

◆ *Will you rebel or live in peace?*

You have been collecting evidence to help you decide whether to rebel against the Normans or whether to live in peace. Remember this may be your last chance. William's sons and their barons are fighting among themselves. What will you decide?

An English lord

A villager from the North of England

A merchant

ACTIVITY B

1 Look at the table you have filled in from page 31. Make a list of
   a) the three best reasons for joining a new rebellion
   b) the three best reasons for not joining a rebellion.
2 Now is the time to take your decision. Use the Rebellion Staircase to help you. Which step on the staircase have you reached? Explain your choice.
3 Which step on the Rebellion Staircase do you think the three people on the right might have reached? Explain the reasons for your decisions.

REBELLION!

4. I will rebel now, whether we win or lose. We must at least try to put an end to all the deaths and destruction. We want freedom!

3. I want to rebel but I will not. We cannot win. The Norman knights and their castles are too strong for us. Look at the way they punished people who rebelled before.

2. I don't like some of the changes since 1066. I would like to have an English king again but getting enough to eat and drink is more important to me than rebelling against the Normans.

1. I know there have been a lot of problems since 1066 but the Normans have changed some things for the better.

ACTIVITY C

1 You have been developing your empathy (understanding of the thoughts and feelings) for people after 1066. Here are three kinds of evidence that have helped you. How many examples can you think of for each kind of evidence?
   a) documents
   b) actions described in documents
   c) non-written sources
2 Which of these statements do you agree with? Explain your choice.
   a) We completely understand how people were thinking and feeling after 1066.
   b) We can get a good idea of people's thoughts and feelings but we can't be certain about them.
   c) We have no real idea what people were thinking and feeling after 1066.

So far in Section 2 you have looked at the dramatic consequences of the Norman Conquest. Consequences are the things that happen as a result of an event. Things such as castle-building, rebellions and terrible punishments were consequences of the Norman Conquest.

The Norman Conquest was significant (or very important) to the people you have studied – the men killed at Hastings; the rebels; the people whose homes were destroyed to make way for castles or after rebellions; and also the Normans who came to England with William, whose lives changed dramatically as well when they settled down to live in England.

However, it's time to ask some different questions before you decide how significant the Norman Conquest really was. We don't just need to know:

◆ what changed; and
◆ who was affected.

We also need to work out:

◆ what did not change (the continuities); and
◆ whether everyone was affected.

So opposite are two criteria for deciding whether the Norman Conquest was really such a significant event. Criteria are reasons for deciding or choosing something. For example, you use criteria when you buy clothes – do they fit, are they the right style and colour, do they make you feel good? The two criteria on the right are helpful for deciding whether any event in history was really significant.

How significant was

1
Did people's daily lives change completely or did many things continue without changing?

> I have to harvest the crops whoever rules the country.

the Norman Conquest?

2

Was everyone affected or just some groups and areas?

> I want this survey to discover everything about my country.

The speakers below give two possible answers to your new question: how significant was the Norman Conquest?

> My name's Dr Continuity. The Norman Conquest was not a very important event even if everybody has heard of it. It did not really affect the way ordinary people lived. It did not change houses, clothing, transport or the work that people did. The Normans did not even invade Scotland or Ireland. Most people were probably more worried about the weather because that affected how much food they had to eat!

Dr Continuity

Professor Change

> Professor Change speaking. I say the Norman Conquest was important. People must have been very worried when they heard about the Battle of Hastings. They had new lords who spoke a different language and they were never sure what these new lords would do to them. The Norman Conquest was important to ordinary people because it must have made them frightened. They didn't know what would happen next.

Think back over the work you did in Unit 2.1 and use the two criteria.
a) Make a list of any evidence you can think of that would support either Professor Change or Dr Continuity.
b) Look at your lists. Which historian do you think is probably right?
c) It will be quite tricky to work out how important the Norman Conquest was! Can you think why?

◆ *Why is this investigation tricky?*

What was your answer to question 1c on page 43? If you said that the sources will make the question tricky then you were spot on! The trouble is, as you have already found out, there aren't many written sources that tell us what we want to know – what people were thinking in the years after the conquest. The diagram below explains why and also shows you how historians try to make up for the lack of written evidence.

What was your answer to question 1c on page 43?

ACTIVITY A

How could Dr Continuity and Professor Change use the sources on this page to support their opinions?

Written sources

The best evidence would be people's thoughts but ordinary people and even landowners and merchants did not write them down. After all, fewer than ten per cent of the people could read and write. There are hardly any records of 1066 and the years afterwards apart from government records. Even English monks were probably too shocked and ashamed by the Norman take-over to write about their defeat.

Alternative 1: People's actions are evidence of their thoughts

This is better! These rebels did not write down what they thought but we know what they did – they rebelled! That's a really good clue to how they felt about the Normans. However, most English people did not rebel. What does that tell us?

Alternative 2: Events and attitudes in the twentieth century

Now this is a surprise! It's all right, the Normans did not use tanks at the Battle of Hastings. However, scenes like this can help us. During the Second World War, the Netherlands was invaded and ruled by a foreign army. The Dutch, just like the English after 1066, were governed by people speaking a foreign language; forced to pay for land they had owned before the invasion; and forced to give food to their conquerors, all after a humiliating defeat. Perhaps a good way of understanding how the English felt after 1066 is by studying how people in the twentieth century felt when their country was occupied by a foreign army.

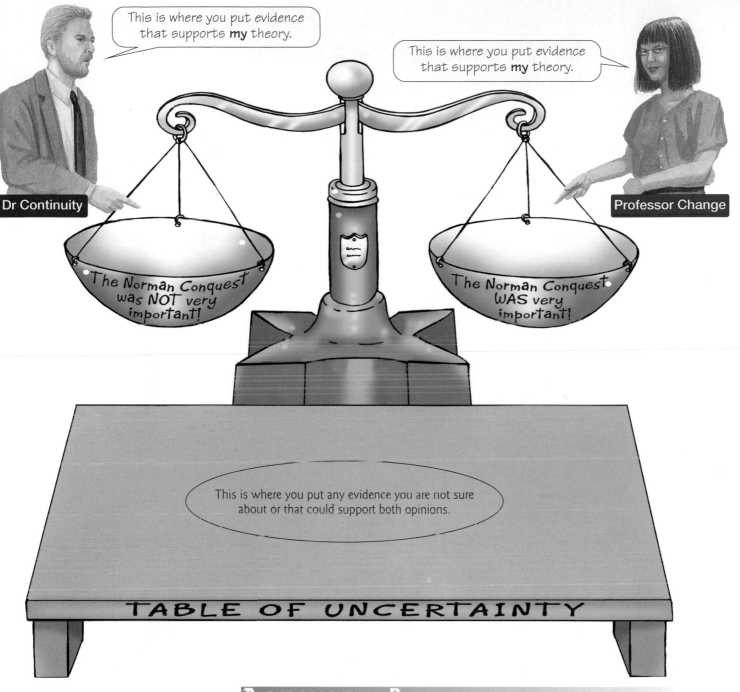

This is where you put evidence that supports **my** theory.

This is where you put evidence that supports **my** theory.

Dr Continuity

Professor Change

The Norman Conquest was NOT very important!

The Norman Conquest WAS very important!

This is where you put any evidence you are not sure about or that could support both opinions.

TABLE OF UNCERTAINTY

ACTIVITY B

On pages 46–49 you will find evidence that will help you decide which of the historians you agree with about the importance of the Norman Conquest. Here's what you do:

1 Draw your own set of scales or get a copy of this one from your teacher.
2 As you work through pages 46–49, answer the questions set by the two historians and add evidence to your scales – or to the Table of Uncertainty!
3 When you have completed your scales diagram, then write your own answer to the question 'Was the Norman Conquest really so important?'

◆ Did the Norman Conquest change people's lives completely?

You already know a little about this topic from page 38. Then you had to find out about some of the changes in people's lives so you could decide whether to rebel. Now you can investigate the same topics for a different reason – to decide whether the Normans really did make a lot of difference to the way people lived. We will also add in some new topics and some new evidence.

> There goes our new lord off hunting. It's fine for him. He won't go hungry anyway. We can do with a plump rabbit for the pot but I don't dare go into the forest with my bow. If I get caught I'll lose my fingers – or worse.

> Best get on with the ploughing then. We still depend on the harvest to have enough to eat. I need to plough my land whether my lord is Norman or Saxon. Normans haven't changed how we farm the land.

> The new Norman bishop at Winchester is building a great new cathedral. I've been ordered to go there to help with the building. I expect I'll have to learn some of their Norman language but that might come in useful.

> After 1066 people still wore the same kinds of clothing and lived in the same types of houses as they did before the Norman Conquest. The new Norman kings and lords were interested in governing England and making themselves rich, not in changing how ordinary people lived.

> I heard people in Winchester have a fancy new fashion. They call their sons after King William's sons, William, Robert and Henry. They say they prefer these new French names to our old Saxon names like Ethelred.

Castles dominated many villages and towns. The English had not built castles like this before 1066.

ACTIVITY

Your task is to work out how the conquest affected each of these topics:

housing   language
cathedrals   transport
lords   castles   dress
farming   medicine
deaths in battle/rebellions
forest laws

Write each topic on one side of the scales – or put it on the Table of Uncertainty if you aren't sure.

The fastest way to travel was still on horseback but most people had to make do with walking. They used oxen to pull their ploughs and carts for carrying heavy weights. The Normans did not make travel faster or introduce any new machines to make work easier.

The Normans used the same medical treatments and cures as the Saxons. They used cures based on herbs that were handed down through families or they used charms and chants to scare away evil spirits.

Can you give us shelter or a bite of food? We've travelled far from the North after the Normans burned our home and killed our menfolk.

I'll do what I can. Our old lord was killed at the great fight at Hastings and we've got a new Norman lord so we have to be careful.

◆ Was everyone affected by the Norman Conquest?

Professor Change

1 Did the Norman Conquest affect **all parts of the country** in the same way?
2 Did the Norman Conquest affect **all classes of people** in the same way?

Dr Continuity

I think this page supports my idea that the Norman Conquest was very important. Can you answer the two questions above and then put your answers onto the correct side of the scales?

Be careful! Don't just agree with her because it's easier than thinking for yourself!

King William has not dared to attack Ireland.

King William claims to rule Scotland but we have our own kings. He has never brought his army to fight us in Scotland.

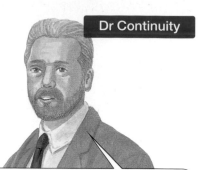

KINGS

SCOTLAND

We tried to rebel but William punished us harshly and now he controls all the North. Everyone here has been affected, rich and poor. The rich lost their lands. William's army destroyed the homes of many ordinary people as a warning not to rebel.

CHIEFTAINS

THE NORTH

The Normans built their castles in south Wales but they have not taken over north Wales.

IRELAND

THE MIDLANDS

William has built his castles all over the South-West. We rebelled but his army was too strong. The rich lost their lands. Ordinary people are afraid of the Norman soldiers even if our daily lives have not changed much.

WALES

PRINCES

THE SOUTH WEST

Our rebellions failed – just like they did in the North. The Norman lords have taken over our land. Everyone here fears them although they do not interfere with our daily lives.

Did the Normans change everything all by themselves?

Professor Change: And now for another great change: cathedrals. The Normans rebuilt all the great cathedrals. They did this to give thanks to God for their victory at Hastings. It was also another way of showing the English people how powerful they were. Look at this page and then write a new sentence for your scales.

Dr Continuity: Don't be so sure! You can't explain every change by saying 'It was the Normans'. It was more complicated than that. The Normans did rebuild the cathedrals but they needed a lot of help – from the weather!
The weather between 1000 and 1300 was very good for farming. The temperature was warm with steady rain at just the right times of year for good harvests. Here's how it worked:

1. This work is costing us a great deal of money but . . .

2. I can afford the building because my church is very wealthy. We own lots of farmland and so . . .

3. We make lots of money because we get good harvests of crops from our land because . . .

4. . . . of our good climate. The harvests make us so much money, which we spend on our cathedral where we give thanks to God for giving us such good weather!

Dr Continuity: And the weather didn't just help build the cathedrals! The higher profits from farming meant that:
1 there was more trade
2 new towns such as Liverpool were started to increase trade
3 ordinary people built stronger houses because they had more money from their own farming.
So the weather had more effect than the Norman Conquest on people's daily lives.

49

Write your own Norman story

Congratulations! You know a lot more about the Norman Conquest than you did a few weeks ago. Now for your final task: can you retell the story of the Norman Conquest? Here it is – the drawings show you what happened – but we haven't written the story to go with the pictures. That's your job!

ACTIVITY

You can use the questions with each picture as a guide but remember:

1 Choose the audience you are writing this for – adults, Year 6 pupils, students your own age in a French school or another choice. Then think about how you will make your words suit your audience.
2 It's up to you what you write – use the questions as a guide, don't just write a series of answers.
3 Make the story as exciting as you like but say what your sources are and whether they are trustworthy.

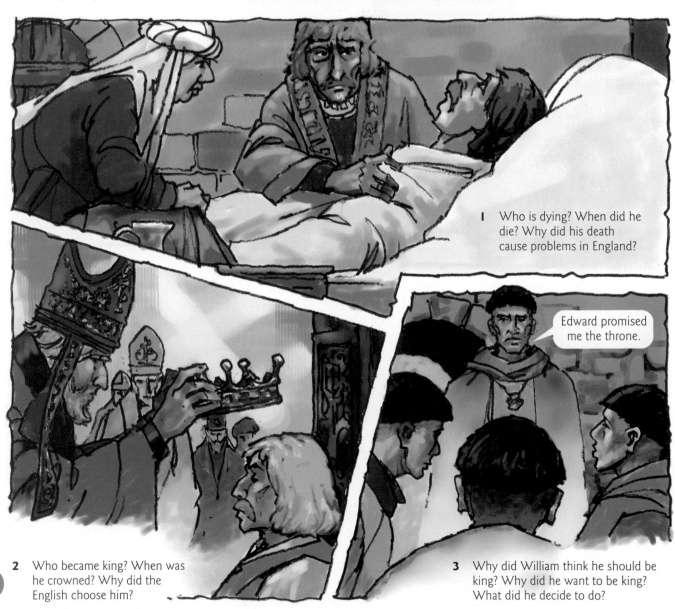

1 Who is dying? When did he die? Why did his death cause problems in England?

Edward promised me the throne.

2 Who became king? When was he crowned? Why did the English choose him?

3 Why did William think he should be king? Why did he want to be king? What did he decide to do?

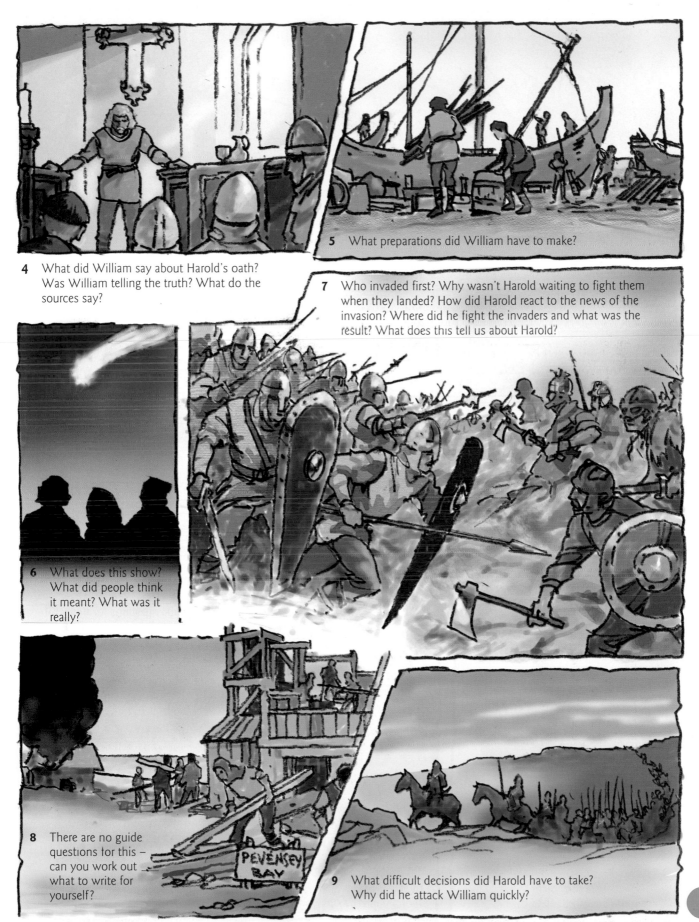

4   What did William say about Harold's oath? Was William telling the truth? What do the sources say?

5   What preparations did William have to make?

6   What does this show? What did people think it meant? What was it really?

7   Who invaded first? Why wasn't Harold waiting to fight them when they landed? How did Harold react to the news of the invasion? Where did he fight the invaders and what was the result? What does this tell us about Harold?

8   There are no guide questions for this – can you work out what to write for yourself?

PEVENSEY BAY

9   What difficult decisions did Harold have to take? Why did he attack William quickly?

10 Who had the best position on the battlefield? Was one army stronger or better-equipped?

11 Did the Normans trick the English? Why is it difficult to decide? Why did the Normans win?

12 There are no guide questions for this – can you work out what to write for yourself?

13 Why did William build castles? Where were they built? What did the English think of them?

14 There are no guide questions for this – can you work out what to write for yourself?

15 How did William punish the northern rebels?
Which sources tell us about the punishments?
How truthful are they likely to be?

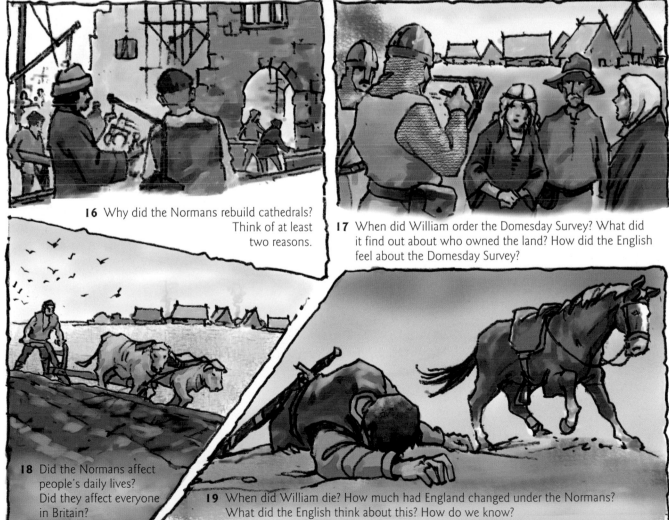

16 Why did the Normans rebuild cathedrals?
Think of at least
two reasons.

17 When did William order the Domesday Survey? What did
it find out about who owned the land? How did the English
feel about the Domesday Survey?

18 Did the Normans affect
people's daily lives?
Did they affect everyone
in Britain?

19 When did William die? How much had England changed under the Normans?
What did the English think about this? How do we know?

Over the next three years you are going to be investigating many more exciting periods and places in history. But would they be so exciting if you could travel back in time to live there? Here's a chance to think about whether you would like to live in the past, in Norman England. Of course, you can't be just anybody because your answer might be different depending on who you were. So first you have to choose (or your teacher will choose for you!) whether you will be

◆ a Norman landowner,
◆ an English merchant, or
◆ an English farm worker.

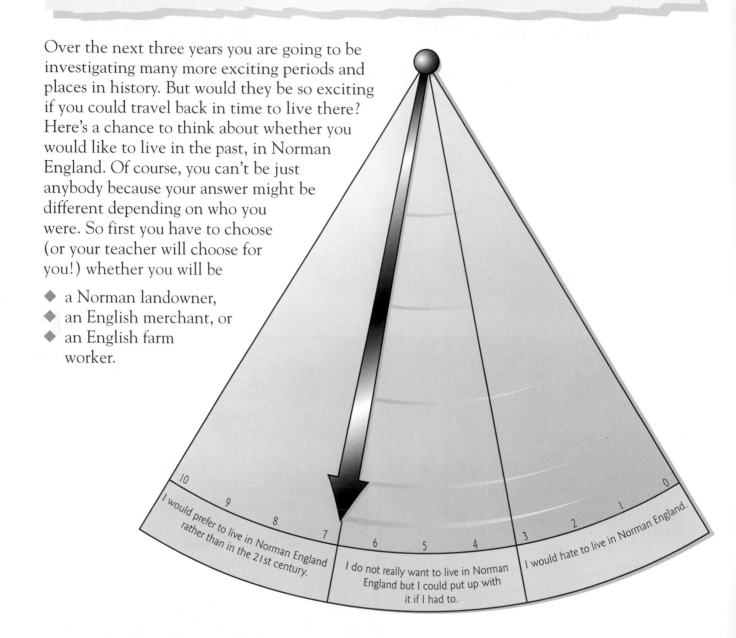

10 9 8 7
I would prefer to live in Norman England rather than in the 21st century.

6 5 4
I do not really want to live in Norman England but I could put up with it if I had to.

3 2 1 0
I would hate to live in Norman England.

ACTIVITY

You are going to use the criteria opposite to decide whether you would like to live in Norman England.

1 Make notes in your own copy of the grid. Give each CRITERION a score out of 10 – a high score if, for example, you think living in Norman England would be comfortable and a low score if you think it would be uncomfortable.

2 Look at all five scores on your grid and work out the average. Now draw your own copy of the pendulum and draw in your arrow showing how keen you are to live in Norman England.

3 Which criterion was most important in making your decision? Explain why.

4 Using the criteria grid for ideas, make a list of the questions you would still like to find answers to about living in Norman England.

SORTING GRID

Criterion 1 How comfortable will I be?

Icon:

Comfort

Food

Drink

Clothing

Light and heat

Housing and furniture

Clean water; toilets

Energy and fuel

Transport

Criterion 2 How much work will I have to do?

Icon:

Work

All day

Part-time

Just at school

Slavery

Rates of pay

Help from machinery

Criterion 3 What can I do for enjoyment?

Icon:

Enjoyment

Games

Sports

Music

Books

Holidays

Visits

Criterion 4 What dangers and suffering will there be?

Icon:

Danger

Crimes

Help from police

Medicines and hospitals

Diseases

Life-expectancy

Criterion 5 How free and equal will I be?

Icon:

Freedom

Are women and men equal?

Can I vote in elections?

Are minorities persecuted?

Are all religions tolerated?

Can you marry whoever you want?

King John William gave his lords lots of land. One hundred years later, William's great-great-grandson John fought the great-great-grandsons of William's lords. The lords won.

'King' Cromwell? William was good at defeating rebels. But in the 1640s some people rebelled against another of William's descendants, King Charles I. They won a Civil War then executed Charles. Their leader, Oliver Cromwell, became the ruler of England although he refused to be called a king.

If William could see into the future, what would catch his attention? Here are some of the things you could well be studying in Key Stage 3 history. What might William have thought about each?

ACTIVITY

All the historical events listed here are different and special. But can you see any **similarities** with the events you have learned about in this book? What are the important **differences**?

Lost in Time William made lots of changes in England, but they were nothing compared to the changes that happened later. What would William have made of factories and steam engines?

Dying for the Vote! William forced people to do what he wanted. What would he have thought of the big change in the nineteenth and early twentieth centuries, when British men and women got the right to choose their own leader?

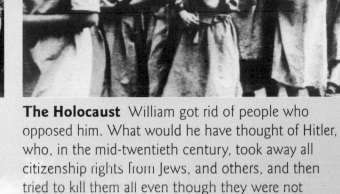

The Holocaust William got rid of people who opposed him. What would he have thought of Hitler, who, in the mid-twentieth century, took away all citizenship rights from Jews, and others, and then tried to kill them all even though they were not actively fighting him?

The Trenches William's battles were small-scale compared to modern warfare. What would he have thought of the four-year First World War involving millions of soldiers and the French and the English fighting on the same side?

Impact of Empire William ruled a Norman Empire, but it was tiny compared with the British Empire. What would William have thought of how, from the seventeenth to the twentieth century, British people crossed the sea to seize land and become rich, creating the massive British Empire?

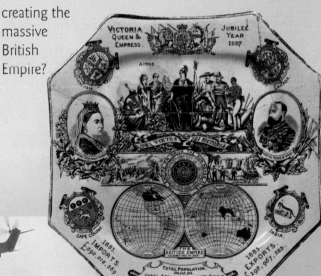

The Twentieth Century
In some ways, a familiar story: war, war and more war. But what else would William have noticed in the twentieth century? What would he have thought was really significant?

◆ Glossary

ANGLO-SAXON	A person of English origin, before the Norman Conquest
ARCHAEOLOGICAL	Concerning excavations which search for remains from the past
BAILEY	The outer section of a castle
BIASED	Unfairly in favour of or against something or someone
COMET	A type of star that moves through space with a visible 'tail' of gas and dust. Centuries ago it was seen as a significant sign, or omen
CORONATION	The ceremony of crowning a new king or queen
CRITERIA (*singular* CRITERION)	Factors to consider when making a decision or choice; standards that something is judged by
FAMINE	A time when people have no food and many die from hunger
HEIR	The next person in line to take over a position, for example, as king or queen of a country
LOOTED	Robbed, stole from
MOTTE	The mound which was the most strongly defended part of a castle
NORMAN	A person from medieval Normandy, in the north of France
OATH	A solemn or official promise
POMMEL	The upright front part of a saddle
SHIRE	A county, such as Yorkshire or Kent

◆ Index

Alfred the Great 31
Anglo-Saxon army: equipment
    12–13
Anglo-Saxon Chronicle 22, 23,
    31
Arques, Battle of 17

Bayeux Tapestry 6–7, 8, 11,
    20–21, 22
British Empire 57

castles 32–33
cathedrals 38, 40, 46, 49
Charles I, King of England 56
Cromwell, Oliver 56

Denmark: alliances with English
    rebels 34
Domesday Book 35, 36–7
Domesday Survey 33, 35, 36
Douglas, Professor D. C. 24

Edric the Wild 34
Edward the Confessor 2, 4, 20

First World War 57
Fulford, Battle of 9, 10

Giffard, Walter 17

Hardraada, Harald 9
Harold, Earl of Wessex (King
    Harold of England) 2–3, 4,
    10–11, 20

claim to the throne 22, 24
death of 16, 17
evaluations of 9, 18
Harrying of the North 34, 35
Hastings, Battle of 2–3, 4
    course of 15–17
    location of 14
    tactics 16, 17
Hereward the Wake 34
Hitler, Adolf 57
Holocaust 57
Ireland 34, 48

John, King of England 56
John of Worcester 22, 23

Kennett, Cambridgeshire 37

Malcolm III of Scotland 19

Norman Conquest
    effects of 38, 42, 43, 46–7, 48–9
    and later history 56–7
    significance of 42–3, 44
Normans
    army equipment 12–13, 33
    castles 3, 32–3, 34
    control of the English 33, 38
    rebellions against 34

Odo, Bishop of Bayeux 6, 7

rebellions
    seventeenth century 56

against the Normans 34
failure of 48
Norman reply to 34, 35, 36
reasons for 38

Scotland 19, 48
Second World War 44
Song of the Battle of
    Hastings 13
sources 5, 44
    English 22–3
    evaluation of 6–7, 21, 23, 26–7
    French 6–7, 20–1
Stamford Bridge, Battle of 9, 10
Swanneck, Edith 17

Vikings 9
Vitalis, Orderic 35
voting rights 57
Wales 48
Waltheof, Earl 34
weather: influence on historical
    events 49
William, Duke of Normandy (King
    William I of England) 2–3,
    4–5, 35, 36
    claim to the throne 20–1
    death of 30
    evaluations of 4, 8, 18, 40
William of Jumièges 24
William of Poitiers 20, 21
writing guidelines 5, 8, 9, 18
    story of the Norman Conquest
    50–3

THIS IS HISTORY!

◆ Titles in the series:

Pupils' Books (PB) and Teachers' Resource Books (TRB) are available for all titles.

Write Your Own Roman Story	**PB** 0 7195 7717 9	**TRB** 0 7195 7718 7
The Norman Conquest	**PB** 0 7195 8555 4	**TRB** 0 7195 8556 2
King John	**PB** 0 7195 8539 2	**TRB** 0 7195 8540 6
Lost in Time	**PB** 0 7195 8557 0	**TRB** 0 7195 8558 9
'King' Cromwell?	**PB** 0 7195 8559 7	**TRB** 0 7195 8560 0
The Impact of Empire	**PB** 0 7195 8561 9	**TRB** 0 7195 8562 7
Dying for the Vote	**PB** 0 7195 8563 5	**TRB** 0 7195 8564 3
The Trenches	**PB** 0 7195 8565 1	**TRB** 0 7195 8566 X
The Holocaust	**PB** 0 7195 7709 8	**TRB** 0 7195 7710 1
The Twentieth Century	**PB** 0 7195 7711 X	**TRB** 0 7195 7712 8

◆ Acknowledgements

Photographs reproduced by kind permission of:

Cover Michael Holford; **p.2** *all* Michael Holford; **p.3** *all* Michael Holford; **p.4** Michael Holford; **p.6** Michael Holford; **p.7** Michael Holford; **p.8** Michael Holford; **p.9** Michael Holford; **p.11** Michael Holford; **p.12** *all* Michael Holford; **p.13** *both* Michael Holford; **p.14** © Copyright Jim Bradbury; **p.15** *all* Michael Holford; **p.16** Michael Holford; **p.17** Michael Holford; **p.20** Michael Holford; **p.22** The British Library; **p.31** The British Library; **p.37** The Public Record Office; **p.42–43** Michael Holford; **p.44** Hulton; **p.56** *tl* Michael Holford, *tc* The British Library, *tr* ASAP/Hulton Deutsch, *br* Mary Evans Picture Library; **p.57** *tl* Mary Evans/Fawcett Library, *tr* Mary Evans Picture Library, *cl* Imperial War Museum, *cr* The Art Archive/Eileen Tweedy, *bl* Katz/Frank Spooner.

(*t* = top, *b* = bottom, *l* = left, *r* = right, *c* = centre)